This book is designed to help American families free themselves from the debt caused by the pandemic and to find financial peace within their future.

Follow along as Derek Nelson teaches you how to reach your financial goals by covering core topics like...

$ Government Spending and why it matters to you.

$ Why it's important to be debt free.

$ How to eliminate debt.

$ How to maximize savings for retirement, college, and beyond.

$ How to create a tax-free nest egg.

For more information on how you can have financial freedom in a post pandemic world Contact Derek Nelson at:

1-727-902-1083   Derek@polarisfinancialnetwork.com

https:/polarisfinancialnetwork.com

Table of Contents

Introduction..1

Chapter One: Federal Government & Debt...............................4

Chapter Two: Potential Tax Increases......................................6

Chapter Three: Our Healthcare System..................................10

Chapter Four: Buy Term & Invest the Difference....................12

Chapter Five: Steps for Financial Peace.................................15

Chapter Six: The Debt Paradigm..23

Chapter Seven: Government Regulated Retirement Accounts......28

Chapter Eight: Big Banks & Wall Street..................................38

Chapter Nine: How Much Do I Need for Retirement?..............43

Chapter Ten: Saving for College...47

Chapter Eleven: Home Ownership...49

Chapter Twelve: But I've Already Built My Nest Egg...............55

Chapter Thirteen: Protection..62

Chapter Fourteen: Final Thoughts..65

Introduction

On March 1st, 2020, I published my first book titled, Financial Foundation System. This was published just as the pandemic was unfolding. In fact, most of us were still going about our business, at least for a few more weeks.

Then all of a sudden, everything changed. The COVID-19 pandemic has been a catastrophe in so many ways for so many of us. Loved ones became sick and even passed away, businesses completely shut down, never to reopen, and **millions of people not prepared financially** for this Black Swan event that hit us, making us feel extremely vulnerable both with our lives and our finances.

As a matter of fact, my family was hit with COVID-19. I was feeling tired the entire week and then on Thursday, started to feel more fatigued and even ill. I went to get a rapid test and came back positive. By the next day, I would have a 101.3, a massive headache, and just felt horrible. Luckily, the fever broke, but for the next several days, I would be battling extreme fatigue, muscle pain, and a nasty cough. In addition, my wife had a very high fever, highest hitting 103.8, and it would persist for almost a week. The following week, my wife would spend several weeks in the hospital as her oxygen levels were low and developed pneumonia. All three of my children also got it, though they had lower fevers. This was certainly a major challenge for us.

I explained black swan events in my previous book, but just in case you didn't read it and are not sure what it is, allow me to explain. A black swan event, according to Investopedia, **is an unpredictable event that is beyond what is normally expected of a situation and has potentially severe consequences.**

Black swan events are rare, unexpected, and can wreak havoc on communities, and even an entire planet, as we recently witnessed.

Some other notable events that would be classified as black swan events are Hurricane Katrina in 2005, Hurricane Harvey in 2017, and even the deep freeze Texas saw in March of 2021.

Why do I open the content of this book with so much negativity? The reason is simple. I want you to be financially prepared for unexpected events. Black swan events are broad and can hit us without warning, often costing people their lives, and billions of dollars.

We also have our very own little mini black swan events over the course of our lives. For example, we could be living our lives, when suddenly, a stroke occurs. If a stroke occurs, and we live, it could mean months of rehabilitation, which also means months of a lost income.

While these events do occur, it should not stop us from achieving financial peace of mind. Financial peace begins with understanding and planning. It is my dream to free millions of Americans from the chains of debt. By doing this, each one of you will be able to maximize your savings and bring yourselves true financial peace.

I had no intention of writing another book, however, since living through COVID-19, and witnessing what so many have gone through, including my own family members, I felt compelled to write once again.

The purpose of this book is to get you to think. I am going to ask a ton of questions, just like I would with a client of mine. In fact, if I ever have the pleasure of working with you, you just may read the questions here and then hear them again when we chat.

I will also talk about different scenarios to help you understand, not only how important a sound financial plan is, but ways to ensure you create one for yourself and for those dearest to you.

The first half of this very quick and easy read will be dedicated to the understanding of financial matters our nation is facing. The second part will be to help you understand your situation and how a simple, yet powerful plan can be implemented to bring you financial peace of mind.

Chapter One: Federal Government & Debt

It is no secret that our country is in debt. Our national debt has been steadily increasing for decades. As a matter of fact, the last president to leave office with a national debt lower than when he entered office was Calvin Coolidge in 1929. In other words, every president since 1929 has implemented policies that increased the national debt.

The real issues we face are that the national debt is not only growing at a disturbing rate, but we now have many, more complex programs that require funding. So, one has to wonder, will our national debt ever decrease, let alone be paid, again? Doesn't the United States, via taxpayer dollars, have to pay the interest on this debt?

As I write this, **our national debt is over $28 trillion!** It is projected that it will be over $51 trillion in 2025, and $90 trillion by 2029! Folks, that's this decade! It really doesn't matter if we have a Republican or Democrat president, does it? The entire government continues to add to our financial problems. This is all going to hit us real hard one day, and I have the feeling this day could be sooner than we think.

There are enormous challenges ahead. Our great nation faces multiple issues, and the government is generally run pretty poorly, which most of us can agree on. Many of these issues and challenges will require money, and a lot of it, to deal with. The question is, where does the government get this money?

The answer to the money question for the past two decades is they will print the money. We continue adding money to the supply and the printing of money is not getting any slower. Doesn't this mean inflation? Won't our dollars buy less while costs of goods and services rise? What will this do to our standard of living?

As I write this, we are in a pandemic. COVID-19 has taken the lives of over 3.87 million globally, as of 6/22/2021, and over 600,000 in the United States alone. Many of us got sick and even had to say goodbye to loved ones. It has been an absolute tragedy for so many families.

What kind of economic impact has the pandemic had? Many small businesses were shut down, people found themselves with no income, and quite frankly, uncertain in some cases, how they would feed their families. **It was evident very early on that this country had a savings problem.** So many found they were reliant on the government sending them money and/or freezing certain payments like auto loans, rents, and mortgages.

Do you know where the government gets the money from? They print and borrow. Will this money ever be paid back or are we simply compounding an unstoppable national debt problem? There will come a time this will have to be dealt with. The question is when? For now, we continue to punt the football down the field, so perhaps someone else in the future can tackle this problem.

Chapter Two: Potential Tax Increases

There are many potential tax increases on the table. At this point in time, tax rates are historically low, and yet, income taxes have a huge impact on our savings efforts and lifestyle choices. **Are you aware that the average American will pay over $525,000 in taxes over a lifetime?** This is roughly a third of everything they make.

New Jersey is among the worst states, when it comes to taxation. Residents pay over $931,000! There are currently 11 states where it costs more than 40% of people's lifetime earnings and 26 states where you will pay more than a third in taxes! Looking at it another way, if you are paying 33% in taxes, work five days a week, and take two weeks off every year, then 83 of the 250 days worked are just to pay taxes. Basically, you are working for the government for 83 days.

Now, let us review some of the potential tax increases we are facing. Keep in mind, none of us are certain which ones will pass immediately, in the near future, or never. The fact that these are on the table should be enough to alarm anyone.

The government is seeking to broaden the Social Security tax of 12.4% (6.2% for employees & 6.2% for employers), which is currently imposed on earned income up to $142,800. What they are seeking is to tax all earned income in excess of $400,000

One of the key benefits for those who invest in real estate is the tax code 1031. What this does is allow investors to use the profits from one property and invest into another, without any tax consequences. This benefit could be eliminated. If you recall, other politicians, including Michael Bloomberg, also mentioned eliminating this tax benefit. What would this do to the real estate market?

Of course, they are seeking to increase income taxes for higher earners. This should come as no surprise to anyone. In fact, if you were to ask me, it is inevitable. The question is will it be enough to simply tax the high earners? Will this fix our massive debt problem, or will the government impose higher income taxes for everyone at some point?

Are you aware that 90% of our population earns less than $100,000 a year? Doesn't this mean there are not nearly enough higher income earners to tackle our growing debt problems? **Won't they have to tax the rest of us at higher rates as well?**

The Biden administration has also proposed eliminating the step up basis at the time of death. This is a massive money grab from the federal government if this were to pass. Allow me to offer you a scenario so you may understand a bit more clearly.

Let's say you have parents that have lived in their home since 1985. They purchased the land and had a house built. You grew up in this home as a child, and today, they still call this house home.

When they pass away, they are going to leave you, their home. You are free to live there, rent it out, or sell it. Naturally, they only want you to do what is best for you and your family.

When they purchased the property and had the home built, it had cost them about $100,000. If they were to pass away today, the home will probably sell for $375,000. When you inherit the home, your cost basis will be $375,000, assuming that was the value at the time of death.

This is a great way for families to help their children and grandchildren get a little head start or injection into their savings plans. Think about it. This could help a family purchase their first home, enhance retirement savings, or even be a source to pay for a child's higher education.

What the government is proposing is that when you inherit this home, your cost basis will be the original $100,000 rather than the $375,000. This means you will be responsible for $275,000 in capital gains taxes!

In other words, your family was diligent in saving, lived frugally, and did everything right, so that they can leave you with something when they are gone. Now the government is looking to take their piece of the pie, because of their mismanagement and misappropriation of trillions of dollars.

This one is the best! Of course, I am being funny, even though it is far from humorous. **The government is considering a cap on how big a retirement account may grow.**

Imagine you do everything right, save every month in your retirement account, build a comfortable nest egg for retirement, and then the government decides you have too much! You read that right! **You could be penalized for saving too much!** This is one of the most disturbing, so-called tax increases, I've read because it directly affects middle America. It also seems like this, among other increases, is an effort to eliminate the middle class all together.

Oh, and just so you are aware, caps on how much your retirement account could grow, was also a discussion during the Obama administration. I feel it is only a matter of time before this is implemented.

We don't know what these penalties/taxes could be. What we do know is that plans such as the 401(k), IRA, & 403(b), are regulated by the government and they can change the rules whenever they want. Please consider saving in an asset class that is all but non-existent in the government's eyes. We will discuss this in a later chapter.

I don't want to bore you with all the other tax hike proposals because I think you get the point. What we need to ask ourselves is will it be enough? With our nation's debt, deficits and massive spending, will they be introducing more, or less, tax increases over the next few years.

Chapter Three: Our Healthcare System

A political debate that has seemed to be raging for the past 20 years is our healthcare system. We saw major changes unfold during the President Obama administration when the Affordable Care Act was passed. Healthcare costs have steadily risen over the past several years and show no sign of slowing down.

Many companies that offer their employees health insurance, are offering high deductible plans. These plans often come with higher premiums and much higher out of pocket expenses. In fact, the average monthly premiums for a family to have health insurance is $1,152 per month. This comes out to be $13,824 a year!

What I can say about our healthcare system is do not expect costs to come back in anytime soon. In fact, health insurance premiums have been steadily rising roughly 7% a year! This means before 2030 rolls in, a family plan, assuming all things remain equal, could be over $25,000 a year! **That's almost double the costs and it's less than 10 years away!**

How will we pay for these benefits? With costs rising the way they are, will employers look to pass more of these costs on to employees? How will families be able to afford health insurance? With the median household income nationally being just over $78,000, healthcare costs could soon be well over 30% of our income. Wage increases, over the past 20 years, have not kept pace with cost of living and the higher these costs rise, the more difficult it will be to save for our own futures.

The other part of our healthcare system is Medicare. Politicians are consistently pushing for changes to Medicare, and some have even called for Medicare for all. Although this may sound noble when we hear it, there is always one question I think of when the government is attempting to push through something like Medicare for all:

Where will we get the money to pay for all of this?

We also hear about how our Social Security system is broken. Don't get me wrong, it is. What we don't hear too much about is how broken our Medicare system is. Afterall, don't we pay for Medicare our entire working lives in the form of taxes as well?

As of July 6, 2021, we are operating at a loss with our Medicare System. In fact, we have an unfunded liability of over $33 trillion! Just in case you need clarity on what an unfunded liability is, here is a simple definition:

Unfunded liabilities are essentially an unfunded project. **In other words, there aren't enough assets to cover the expenses.** In 2029, which is this decade, the unfunded liability for Medicare is forecasted to top $50 trillion. This of course, if the program is not changed.

What if it is changed? What would happen to our debt, unfunded liabilities, and even personal taxes if they were to lower the Medicare eligibility age to 60, as an example? Won't this instantly put millions of more people on Medicare? Who will pay for this? Won't this accelerate the rising costs of healthcare across the board? Where will we get the money to pay for all of this?

I ask these questions over and over because I want you to understand what could potentially happen down the road. By the way, when I say down the road, I'm not talking 30 years from now. We could actually see some major changes within this decade!

Chapter Four: Buy Term & Invest the Difference

Buy term and invest the difference is a popular strategy that is pushed by certain insurance entities, along with a couple of unlicensed entertainers. The idea behind it is that term insurance would cost a fraction of what a permanent policy would cost and that the difference in cost could be invested into mutual funds.

This strategy became popular in the 1970's by a man named Arthur Williams. He founded a company called A.L. Williams, which would later become Primerica.

I truly believe this became more of a marketing plan, rather than a financial plan. Does it really make sense to implement such a plan? Well, if you believe entertainers, like Dave Ramsey, who have been heard saying mutual funds return 12%, then you may be likely to buy into this kind of strategy.

Mutual fund returns are often misleading. The way they calculate them and the returns the mutual fund investor would see, are two very different things. Let me give you a quick example:

Year	Mutual Fund	Starting Balance	Ending Balance
1	+100%	$10,000	$20,000
2	-50%	$20,000	$10,000
3	+100%	$10,000	$20,000
4	-50%	$20,000	$10,000

If you do the math on the mutual fund performance, you will come up with an average return of 25%. However, because of the sequence of returns, **you earn absolutely zero!** In fact, you would have less money because we aren't even factoring in fees.

This is a very deceptive practice. Maybe Dave was right when he said funds can average 12%. Just realize it has nothing to do with the returns you may or may not see.

On a side note, I am not against term insurance. In fact, I own some myself just to ensure there is enough life insurance should something happen to me. I just believe that term insurance shouldn't be the only life insurance owned, and I'll explain why.

I recently had a conversation with someone, we will call him Fred, who had a $1,000,000 term policy set to expire. He had taken out the policy at age 40, and now at age 60, his 20 year term was up.

Could Fred keep this policy if he continues paying the premiums? Yes, he can. The problem with this is that the premium price was **only guaranteed for 20 years.** After that, it renews every year based on age.

His premiums were $113.69 a month. In year 21, **the insurance company can charge him up to $1,840 a month!** Now, this doesn't mean they will, but they legally can. Then every year it resets, and the premiums can, and most likely, will be higher than the previous year.

Since he was 60 years old and still in good health, he could qualify for a new policy. He was interested in a new, 20 year term, that would take him to age 80. A million dollar policy at age 60, would cost him over $793 a month! Even if he took half the insurance, a $500,000 policy, it would still run him $406 a month.

You see, 20 years ago, he had bought into the buy term and invest the difference concept. Fast forward to today, he not only realizes the importance of life insurance for his family, but he didn't do a great job of investing the difference.

Consider this though. What if you only have a term, run into some major health complications, and are unable to obtain life insurance later in life? What will happen to your loved ones if you leave them nothing but medical bills?

If a 40 year old were to obtain a million dollar policy, but have permanent insurance included, they would be much better off in the long run. Allow me to demonstrate what I mean.

With the above, Fred paid a total of $27,285.60 over 20 years. After outliving the policy, he had nothing to show for it. If he were to take out another 20 year term, to take him to age 80, a $500,000 policy would cost him an additional $97,440. This comes out to a total of $124,725.60 in premiums and after age 80, will again, have nothing to show for it.

If Fred were to do a blend of whole life and term, this is what it would look like. He could have bought a million dollar plan for $397.04 a month at age 40. This would have been about $200,000 for a whole life and $800,000 for a 20 year term.

At age 60, the term would drop off and he would be done paying into the whole life policy. His total premiums would add up to $95,289.60. The difference is not only with total cost, but also the fact that Fred has insurance & cash value for life.

In fact, when he is 60, he will now have $307,000 in death benefit and $103,000 in cash value. At age 70, without paying another dime into the policy, Fred could have $374,000 in death benefit and $168,000 in cash value. If he should live beyond age 80, both his death benefit and cash value will continue to grow.

I would also like to point out that if Fred wanted to during the years he had the 20 year term policy, he could have at any time, **converted the policy into a cash value plan.** This would ensure, not only permanent death benefit, but more savings he could access at any time.

There are many other benefits associated with permanent life insurance. In the following chapters, the many ways to utilize life insurance, while alive I might add, will be revealed to you. So, are you ready? Let's continue.

Chapter Five: Steps for Financial Peace

Creating financial peace of mind may seem like a daunting task right now. You might be wondering how to get out of debt or perhaps you are concerned about saving enough for the future. Believe me when I say this. You are far from alone. **We are all overspending somewhere and sometimes all it takes is another pair of eyes to make sense of it.**

In this chapter, I will outline simple steps to take so that you can enjoy that financial peace of mind you have been seeking for so long. While I will list these steps in linear fashion, I also understand that everyone's situation and concerns are unique. So, please don't see this as a one size fits all approach, but rather a guideline. Okay, here we go.

Step One: Identify

When I say identify, I mean literally just that. What is your net income? Are you paying enough in taxes or are you paying too much? The simple way to know this is by reviewing your past returns. Do you typically get a refund, or do you always seem to owe money?

The biggest thing we must all identify is located on the expense side. Does the money fly out of your checking account as quickly as you get it? Do you sometimes wonder if there will be any money left over at the end of the month?

What are the monthly expenses? Have you really sat down and figured out what goods and services are costing you every month? I would begin with fixed expenses. Some examples of fixed, or almost fixed monthly expenses could be:

- Electric bill
- Water bill
- Cell phone bill
- Auto insurance bill
- Mortgage/Rent payment
- Life insurance

Once this number is determined, we can then move on to the other expenses. These items generally include:

- Credit Cards
- Auto loans
- Personal loans
- Student loans

Step 2: Find the Money

Okay, I can hear you through this book right now thinking, "but Derek, I have all these credit cards and other bills. I just don't have any extra money." Believe me, I get it. None of us has any extra money. Things are expensive and prices continue to rise before our very eyes.

What we need to do is get creative. For example, do you often get a refund come tax time? If you answered yes to this, then finding the money is super easy. Simply adjust your withholdings so that less taxes come out of your check every pay period.

I know it seems nice to get that lump sum deposited into your account every April but consider this. What if, instead of a refund, you eliminated $200, $500, or even $1,000 a month in credit card payments? How much further along would you be? Think you could accumulate your savings a little faster if these bills were eliminated? Of course, you could! That's why you are taking the time to read this.

Something else to consider. When you are overpaying the Internal Revenue Service, they are holding onto your money and paying you absolutely zero. While offering them an interest free loan, way too many of us often rack up credit cards during the year and are paying double digit interest. Then we get our refund check, allocate a portion of it to pay down the cards, only to repeat the cycle. I am here to say, the cycle stops now!

There are many ways we can find money to help us, not only to pay off debts, but to also enhance our savings efforts. Here are some examples:

- Cease contributing to retirement savings until debts are paid
- Use the equity in your home to pay down credit cards
- Refinance mortgage to a lower interest rate
- Roll credit card debt into another card with a lower interest rate
- Raise deductibles on home and auto insurance
- Shop home and auto insurance for a lower rate

By the way, I am located in Florida and have contacts in several states. If you need me to connect you with someone to help with the mortgage or home and auto insurance, just reach out. I will do my absolute best to make sure you have someone reputable.

Step 3: Protect

It is no secret that we want to protect what matters most. We have insurance on our automobiles, homes, and even our phones. If you think about it though, what is our biggest asset? My answer to this question is your ability to earn an income.

While our ability to produce an income is considered our most valuable asset, it is often grossly under insured. I believe the number one reason people don't carry enough insurance is because of what they think it might cost. The thing is, when we can find the money, affordability should be of no issue.

So, just like we would protect our vehicle and home, we use insurance to protect our income. Although there are a few other ways, the main two types of insurance we use to help protect people's incomes are disability and life insurance.

Life insurance can, not only protect future paychecks, but it can accomplish so much more. For example, the proceeds from a life insurance plan could be used to:

- Replace all income that was meant to be earned
- Pay off credit cards & auto loans
- Pay the mortgage off so your family can continue to live in the home
- Cover funeral costs
- Pay for college expenses

These are a few of the many ways life insurance can help your family, should you, or your spouse pass away unexpectedly. Wouldn't this help you achieve peace of mind, knowing that if a tragedy occurred, your loved ones will be okay, financially speaking.

But what happens if you are involved in a tragedy, like a bad car accident, and survive? You miraculously survive but now require countless surgeries and rehabilitation. Wouldn't this also cause your paycheck to stop? **Medical bills are the number one cause of bankruptcies and foreclosures in this country.** So, how do we prevent an accident or major illness from decimating our lives?

This is where disability insurance comes into play. I know what you are thinking already. You have it through work. Many people do have life and disability through their employer but let us dive into this a bit.

When it comes to employer benefits, a disability plan is often limited. For example, roughly 78% of employers offer their employees only short term disability. When I say short term, I am referring to a benefit that will pay out for up to 2 years.

What happens if you cannot get back into the workforce within 2 years? Are you aware that the average disability lasts just over 2.5 years? What if you were not able to work for 3, 4, or could never go back to work? How will this affect your family financially?

To complicate things even further, short term disability, through an employer, generally only covers 50%-60% of your paycheck, and these benefits are most likely taxed. The reason the benefits are taxed is because the premiums are paid for by the employer. Now, there are plans where there is cost sharing involved, and if the employee contributes to premiums with after tax dollars, then only the employer contribution part of it will be taxed.

If you are one of the many people working and only have an employer sponsored disability plan, I must ask you this. **Can you afford to take a 40%-50% pay cut?** In other words, if your gross paycheck is $4,000 a month, it may be reduced to $2,000-$2,400 a month, and that is before taxes!

This is where a personally owned disability plan can help. One does not necessarily need to cover their entire income with a personally owned disability plan, if they have employer coverage. What you would most likely want to do is get a policy that will cover the difference.

One of the main benefits of owning a personal disability plan is that, unlike an employer paid plan, the benefits that you would receive are distributed to you tax free. This will help recover most, if not all, your lost income, should you ever be in the unfortunate position of not being able to produce a paycheck.

Step 4: Save

We all know that we should be saving our money. We understand that eventually, we will not be working, and hopefully enjoying our retirement years. The most typical ways we save are through government regulated retirement plans such as the 401(k), 403(b), IRA, etc.

I also believe that we should have access to our funds, should an emergency or opportunity arise. When it comes to government regulated plans, the person taking money out prior to retirement, could be faced with taxation and penalties.

Yes, you just might have to pay a 10% IRS penalty for accessing your own money, even if for a time of need. We will be discussing this in a later chapter.

Saving sooner rather than later is vital to one's ability to have enough come retirement. A question I ask of people I am speaking with that grabs a lot of attention is this:

"If you were out of work for the next 30 years and weren't producing a paycheck, would that affect you and your loved ones?" After they respond with a yes, which is always, I follow up with this. **"Isn't that what retirement is?"**

The beautiful thing about working with someone like myself is, I work to find the money. Money you didn't even realize you may have had. For example, when we identify the income and expenses, we may find a client that is paying several hundred dollars a month to make minimum credit card payments, has 2 auto loans, along with all their other bills.

A real life example I had recently was a couple, where the husband was contributing $600 a month into a 401(k), while they had over $800 a month being paid out to credit cards. After making a few moves and ceasing the 401(k) contributions, they got their credit cards paid off in a fraction of the time, and for a fraction of the costs!

Some people would scoff at the idea of not contributing to their retirement plan and redirecting it toward debt payoff. Think about it this way, what is the purpose of trying to chase a 3-6% return in the market while paying out double digit interest to the credit card companies? This is just a recipe to ensure you don't have enough saved for later.

Besides, after paying down the credit cards, then the auto loans, they were able to save almost $2,000 a month! While the husband continued to save the $600 in his 401(k) plan, we set up another savings vehicle for them that they had never even considered to be an option.

That option was a **properly structured cash value life policy.** Very few people consider this as a savings vehicle because they have been demonized by Wall St. and unlicensed entertainers.

But here's what I know. When done correctly, a cash value life plan has these benefits:

- Grow money with no downside risk
- Create a completely tax free retirement source
- No IRS restrictions or penalties
- No caps on how much you can contribute
- No effect on a child's ability to qualify for financial aid
- Generally, creditor and lawsuit protected

These are just some of the benefits that cash value life insurance has to offer. In the following chapters, you will read about other real scenarios and concepts, but for now, the most important thing is to help you maximize your savings.

Although these steps were outlined in linear fashion, they are fluid. What I mean by that is, depending on your situation, steps can be done simultaneously. To give an example, you may have overwhelming credit card debt. While now is the time to work on being debt free and not saving, it is imperative that you maintain enough life insurance to protect your family.

On the flip side, maybe your only debts are auto loans. If this is the case, we can build a savings plan as we accelerate these payments, along with making sure you are properly protected.

Everyone's situation is unique and until someone fully understands your situation, it is impossible for them to provide you with solutions.

Chapter Six: The Debt Paradigm

We live in a society, and have for many decades, that is consumer driven. As a result of this, there is tremendous competition for our attention from companies in all industries. Whether you are on social media, watching the television, YouTube, or listening to your favorite radio station, expect to be bombarded with advertisements.

Think about it for a moment. How many times have you seen a Liberty Mutual, or Progressive Insurance ad? What about food advertisements? Sometimes I feel like every other ad is about food. Then there are the automobile dealerships attempting to get you to their location for the best deal of the year, or zero down for your next living room set.

Point is all these advertisements are running with a sole purpose in mind. To get you to spend money and spend it with them. Want to know what? They do an amazing job at it. They understand psychology and that the constant bombardment will break so many of us down and pique our interest.

As of this writing, in 2021, we are a country with an insurmountable debt problem. Household after household is plagued by debt, and for the majority, not even sure how they got so deep into it.

It is no wonder how so many people are behind on their retirement savings. We are too busy trying to get that next best thing, new car, and phone. We must have the latest and greatest and we often are not considering the overall costs.

We are conditioned to get money, both earned and borrowed, get the things we want, then bank a little money, so we can spend that later. It is a cycle that can potentially lead to financial devastation.

We all know that government spending is out of control, but our spending is also out of control at times.

Total personal debt in our country is approaching $22 trillion! Now, just so you understand, mortgage debt is about $17 trillion of this. While I am not too concerned about mortgage debt, I am concerned about how many people may be overextending or paying too much for their homes.

Next in line, and it should be of no surprise to anyone, is student loan debt. Student loan debt is steadily approaching $2 trillion with no sign of slowing down. Student loans are another major factor that is inhibiting people to save the way they should be.

Then there is credit card debt. Believe it or not, as I write this, the national credit card debt is slowly declining. Don't get me wrong, it is still about $1 trillion. When we look more toward per household, the average debt is right around $16,000 and the average interest rate is 16.72%. Allow me to illustrate an example of a typical way we pay our credit cards.

Credit Card	Balance	Interest Rate	Monthly Payment
Chase	$5,000	16%	$150
Visa	$6,000	24.99%	$180
Capital One	$5,000	10.99%	$150
Totals:	$16,000	17.32%(Approx.)	$480

Companies, balances, interest rates, and payments are for illustration purposes only

In the above example, we are showing a monthly payment of 3% of the total balance, which adds up to $480 a month. If the payments were to continue at this pace, it would take nearly 27 years to pay off and cost $18,688 in interest!

By simply rearranging how we pay these cards, not even allocating more money toward paying them, we can reduce the time it takes to pay them to about 4 years and save $11,972 in interest paid!

If we were to take it a step further and add $200 a month to paying off the cards, then we could be credit card free in under 2 years, pay $3,471 in interest, rather than $18,688 or even

$11,972, and have the peace of mind that comes along with being able to now save $680/month! Wouldn't it be nice to have an extra $200, $400, or even $1,000 every month?

Another widely carried debt are automobile loans. Auto loan debt is right around $1.4 trillion. This should come as no surprise as we have been well programmed to purchase on payment, rather than price. Heck, we even buy our phones on payment these days.

The average vehicle is over $41,000! The average interest rate on auto loans is 5.27%. This means that someone with great credit, may qualify for a rate as low as 2% while someone with not so good credit could pay north of 10% interest.

Also, to lower our car payments, we have options as far as how long we would like to take, when it comes to paying off that loan. The average loan length is 72 months. **What most of us are not considering are the overall costs and how much this could be affecting our savings efforts.** Let us look at how much money we might be wasting on our vehicles.

Loan Amount	Length of Loan	Interest Rate	Monthly Payment	Total Cost
$20,000	72 months	5.27%	$324.61	$23,371.92
$40,000	72 months	5.27%	$649.22	$46,743.83
$60,000	72 months	5.27%	$973.83	$70,115.76

Numbers for illustration purposes only

I know you are familiar with APR, which stands for Annual Percentage Rate, but do you truly understand it? APR is the annual rate charged for borrowing the funds. What lenders do is add on different costs associated with the loan. This makes an interest rate of 5.27%, not only not the real interest rate, but a deceptive practice as well, in my mind.

Let me explain what I am referring to. If you have a $40,000 loan, based on the above chart, it is going to cost you $46,743.83 in total. This makes the real interest rate 16.9%!

The way I figure this out is by dividing the interest paid, $6,743.83 by the amount borrowed, $40,000. **You would pay 16.9% more than what you borrowed.**

Now imagine if it were someone whose credit score was lower, and their interest rate was 10.99%. This would mean that their monthly payment would go from $649.22 to $761.16 a month. This is an additional $111.94 a month. Now, on the surface, it may not seem so bad, and this is exactly why dealerships sell on payment, not price.

By paying the additional $111.94 every month, you increase the total costs to $54,803.52! This is an extra $8,059.69 out of pocket and the real interest rate becomes 37%! Can you say wow!

Over time, if you finance just three $40,000 vehicles at 5.27%, it will cost $140,231.49. However, there is more to the story. What is the real cost? What is the cost of not saving $649.22 a month over 18 years? I use 18 years as this is the equivalent of three 72 month loans.

This is where a properly structured cash value life insurance policy can come into play. If a 40 year old were to save the $649.22 rather than spend it, he or she would save $140,238 over 18 years. In the 18th year, the projected account value would be over $196,000. When they turn 65, the account is projected to be over $283,000, despite not contributing another penny.

If this were all to the story, it would be well worth your time to look into this. What if I told you that you could have your cake and eat it too? Are you aware that you can borrow from your plan for any reason, without any government restrictions, or having to qualify?

What I am about to tell you is worthy of your consideration. If this person has been saving in their cash value life insurance plan, rather than spending the money, they could essentially become their own banker.

You see, even if you purchased three $40,000 vehicles outright, you would still be out $120,000. By financing them at 5.27%, you are out $140,231.49. By borrowing from the cash value life plan, you are able to recoup, most, if not all the money. So, what I am telling you is you could borrow $120,000 over time, pay yourself back, rather than a lender, keep that $120,000, plus interest, in your family.

Something else to consider when borrowing from your policy. If you have a real financial situation and cannot make a payment for a few months, nobody is going to show up and repossess your vehicle. This also means it is important to be disciplined and to treat it as if you were paying a lender. Your future self will thank you for all the sound financial decisions you made during your working years.

It is super important to shift the way we think about money. It is designed to flow and circulate. This is exactly what banks do, so why shouldn't we do the same? It is time to grab our finances by the horns, pay down credit cards and other loans we may have out there. It will offer tremendous financial peace of mind and greatly enhance your savings efforts.

I have a question I often ask my clients, and it is a no brainer once you hear it:

Is the money better off in your pocket, or theirs?

Chapter Seven: Government Regulated Retirement Accounts

When I am working with new clients, all too often, they don't understand that the money in their 401(k), 403(b), IRA, or some other retirement account, is not 100% theirs. In fact, I liken it to having a mortgage, or lien on the account. Allow me to explain.

You see, when one is contributing to one of these accounts, they are using before tax dollars. What I mean is generally, the funds come directly out of your paycheck, before the money is taxed.

On the surface, this seems like a smart idea. Money is saved in taxes every year, and because the funds do not get taxed until much later, it grows, what we call, tax deferred. Many see this growth as compound growth and their retirement nest eggs can grow much more efficiently this way.

As we dig deeper however, we realize this may not be ideal. After all, aren't we also deferring our taxes? Won't the taxes be due at some point? How much will we owe?

Government regulated retirement accounts, like a 401(k), are one of the only things Americans purchase without knowing anything about. Think about it. When it is time to get a new automobile, what do we do? We research it. In fact, we consider everything from safety to gas mileage, and 50 things in between.

Recently, my wife and I purchased a new mattress. We went to the store, laid down on several different styles to test their comfort and firmness. When we made our decision, which was the one that made her happiest of course, we sat down with the salesman to write it up. Guess what, we knew exactly what the price was going to be before giving him the payment.

Think about it for a moment. Let's take the 401(k), since this is by far the most popular type of retirement plan. What are the administrative fees? Are there mutual fund fees? What will taxes be down the road?

Now concerning administrative and mutual fund fees, one can determine the costs of the account. That is pretty simple, though they like to bury these costs deep within the paperwork. However, rarely does someone actually take the time to investigate these costs.

When it comes to taxes, we have no idea what future rates will be. What if you are in a higher tax bracket come retirement? I know the saying. "When I'm retired, I will be in a lower tax bracket." Do you really believe that? Are you planning on living on much less income?

The reason I say much less income is because the phrase, "when I'm retired, I will be in a lower tax bracket," was coined somewhere around 1980. Do you know how many different tax brackets there were in 1980? There were 16 of them! As of this writing in 2021, we have only 7.

What this means is if a married couple, filing jointly, is earning $80,000 a year, that would put them in the 12% tax bracket. If this same couple retires and their income is only $60,000 a year, they will remain in the 12% tax bracket. So, it is unlikely that one would end up in a lower tax bracket.

On the flip side, could taxes be higher down the road? When I ask people this question, the overwhelming majority answer is yes. People believe that they could be much higher in fact.

Aren't we potentially creating a tax problem for ourselves down the road? **Could the Internal Revenue Service ultimately be the single largest beneficiary of our lifetime savings?** Unfortunately, that answer is yes.

This is why I say retirement plans have liens on them. There is no escaping taxes when it comes time to take distributions. Let me tell you this little story I heard from a friend of mine.

Many years ago, an IRS agent pulled up to a farm in a rural area. It was very early in the morning, and the farmer was still in his home preparing for his busy day. The agent knocked on the door and the farmer politely let him in.

They had coffee, exchanged pleasantries, and after several moments, the farmer asked, "what brings you out here so early?"

The IRS agent got really quiet and serious for a moment, took another sip of his coffee before setting the mug on the kitchen table. Then he said, "I wanted to catch you before you got on with your day because I have a very important question to ask of you."

The farmer replied, "Okay, ask away."

The agent then asked, "Here is the question, think about it really good, because I am only going to ask this one time.

Would you rather pay your taxes on the seeds you plant or on the harvest you reap?"

The farmer did not need more than ten seconds before answering, "why the seeds of course."

The agent, being fully satisfied with his answer, stood up, shook the farmer's hand, and headed out.

When you consider the 401(k), and other regulated retirement accounts, aren't those retirement accounts being taxed on the harvest? Are you aware that this is what is happening? The Internal Revenue Service, in some cases, could own more than a third of your account. I don't know about you, but I never asked for a business partner for my savings. I especially do not want a partner that contributes zero and then takes a third or more of my money down the road.

I want to discuss a young couple, in their thirties, just getting started as a family. This couple, we will call them Dan and Sally, live pretty typical lives. Dan is an electrician and Sally a nurse.

Dan earns just under $60,000 a year and Sally earns about $65,000. Together, they have over $120,000 in income and are each contributing to their employer sponsored retirement plans.

Both Dan and Sally allocate 10% of their salaries to their retirement plans, and between the two of them, are putting away $12,000 per year. They figure if they do this for the next 25-30 years, get good stock market returns, along with an employer match, they will have enough to retire on.

According to some calculations, between contributions, employer and their own, and market growth, they have estimated that they will have just over $1,000,000 in their nest egg. On top of this, it is their intention to pay down the mortgage by the time they reach retirement age, eliminating that payment.

Dan and Sally are diligent and well thought out. They have an actual plan in place and are doing all the right things, so they think. There are some factors they are not taking into consideration.

One of the most overlooked potential retirement planning risks are market returns. While there is no way to predict how the markets will perform over the long term, we all accept there will be up years and there will be down years.

As a society, saving our hard earned money for the future, when did we decide it was normal to lose 20, 30, or even 50% of our money in order to grow our savings? Why are we okay with taking a major financial hit, even if just on paper, in order to build.

Financial professionals will have many talking points when it comes to down markets. They will advise that these losses are just on paper, and it is never an actual loss, unless we sell.

This advice would be false. What they are not taking into consideration, when statements like these are made, is a little thing called inflation. Inflation erodes our purchasing power over time and if our dollars are not earning, they are losing.

Let me put it this way. If inflation is 3%, then a dollar today is worth $.97 this time next year. In five years, that same dollar would only be worth $.85. Now compound this with some market losses, and this can have a significant impact on retirement savings plans.

Another thing is, what if a downturn in the market occurred closer to retirement? What if it were a major recession developing just a year or two prior to their scheduled retirement date? How would this affect their plans?

Are you aware that the S&P 500 lost about 50% of its value between 2007-2009? What if it were time to retire and this happened? Imagine Dan and Sally, working all those years, saving so diligently, getting to that million dollar goal they set 30 years ago, and then bam! Just like that, one million becomes $500,000. What kind of effect will this have on people's ability to retire?

Now, some people feel $500,000 is a lot of money, and it is. Where we run into problems is how much income we can take without sacrificing the principal. Did you know the number one fear of retirees is running out of money?

Think about it, we are living longer than ever, but at the same time, medical costs continue to rise, even faster than what they tell us inflation is. In fact, the average retired couple, age

65 in 2021, can reasonably expect to have over $300,000 in medical expenses during retirement years. How will they pay for all of this?

You know, if we were to retire at age 65 and live to age 73, we would have no problem planning for retirement. What if you live to age 90, 95, or even 100? What happens if you have a long retirement but run out of money at age 79? What would you do? How will you live?

We are living longer, which means we must plan accordingly. Do you know what someone's largest retirement expense typically is? Would you be surprised to know it is housing? I'm here to help you think. If you think about, and come up with some answers, won't you be able to put yourself in a better position over the long term?

There is another time bomb Dan and Sally are not considering, and that is taxes. You see, we are often told by plan administrators, tax preparers, CPAs, and unlicensed entertainers, that we are compounding our growth because we are deferring paying our taxes. In fact, we are saving money in taxes today! But is this really the case?

If Dan and Sally are contributing $12,000 a year into their 401(k) accounts, they are using before tax money. This means that their taxable income is reduced from $120,000 to $108,000.

Let us say their overall tax rate is 20%, between federal and state taxes. This would save them $2,400 a year. Now, all things being equal, if they do this for the next 30 years, they will save $72,000 in taxes. This is one of the most attractive, so called benefits, of retirement plans, such as a 401(k).

I say so called benefits because, what Dan and Sally do not realize, is that there is a lien on their retirement accounts. Eventually, the taxes saved today will have to be paid. Remember the farmer who chose to pay his taxes on the seeds?

Most of the people we work with agree taxes will be higher in the future. Are you aware they are at historic lows today? In fact, here is a table, illustrating the history of federal income tax rates:

Year	Federal Income Tax Rate
1920	27%
1930	16%
1940	40%
1950	69%
1960	56%
1970	48%
1980	43%
1990	28%
2000	15%
2010	15%
2020	12%

These numbers are based on married couples, filing jointly, earning over $40,000 a year. Keep in mind, these are the tax rates they end up in, not necessarily the percentages they are taxed on all income, as we are in a progressive tax system. In other words, the more you earn, the higher rates you pay.

Okay, back to Dan and Sally. They managed to save $72,000 in taxes over 30 years. As you can see in the table of tax rates, we are at historic lows currently. For now, let us assume they will pay the same 20% in total income tax in retirement.

Dan and Sally happened to fare very well in building their nest egg. They got to the million dollars mark they set out to do thirty years ago. Now it is time to take income from their nest egg so they may live a comfortable retirement.

According to many financial professionals, taking 4% of savings is a comfortable number to help avoid running out of money, so let's use that.

If they saved a million dollars and took out 4% a year, that would be a $40,000 annual income. For starters, is this not drastically reducing their lifestyle? After all, they had been earning about $120,000 a year and are now expected to live on a third of that?

But hey! Let's be fair and say they each receive $2,000 a month in Social Security which gives them an extra $48,000 annually. Now they have $88,000 a year income. They still fall short of the $120,000, but they paid their mortgage off, kids are out of the house, so they are comfortable with this.

On the $40,000 of income, they are taking from their savings every year, every penny they take is taxed. This means at 20%, they will pay $8,000 a year in income taxes, leaving them with $32,000 in income from their savings.

In just ten years' time, they will pay $80,000 in income taxes, and in 25 years, they would have paid $200,000 in income taxes! Keep in mind that over their 30 years of saving, they only saved $72,000 in taxes.
Who does this sound like a better retirement plan for? Dan and Sally, or Federal and State governments?

As an alternative, Dan and Sally could redirect their savings into a properly structured life insurance plan. By doing this, they eliminate a couple of things and gain so much more.

The first thing they eliminate is market risk. The markets go up and down, and we literally have no control over this risk, if that is where our money is. By the way, if you have a 401(k), IRA, or another government regulated retirement plan, aren't your dollars invested in mutual funds? Don't mutual funds invest in company shares that are on various stock markets?

Another potential wealth time bomb that would be eliminated are taxes. While it is true that investing in a Roth account, rather than a traditional retirement plan will accomplish this, Roth accounts still come with market risk. Also, keep in mind that the government is considering placing limits on how much money can be invested in these accounts.

What Dan & Sally will gain by contributing to a cash value life plan is systematic growth. **Their account value will never go down in value and they will know they will have that money to count on down the road.**

So, how does a properly structured cash value life insurance plan grow? It is rather simple. With most plans, they grow by earning interest and dividends. Though dividends are not guaranteed, there are companies that have not missed a dividend payment in over 100 years! They have paid dividends through the best and worst of times, including the Great Depression.

There is a rider, known as Waiver of Premium, that allows the policy to self-fund in the event of a total disability. So, if you ever had to battle a major illness like cancer, or were involved in a major automobile accident, there is a really strong possibility that you will not be working or be able to produce a paycheck. **Waiver of Premium ensures that your plan continues, even if you cannot personally contribute.**

In addition, if something catastrophic happens, like a pandemic, you have access to the cash value in your policy. Wouldn't it have brought some financial peace of mind if you had a savings plan that not only was growing in value, but allowed you access to those funds, with no government restrictions or penalties. This is also useful in the event of a job loss, emergency, like needing a new appliance unexpectedly, or even paying for a family trip.

If this was all there was, it would be a no brainer, but in the voice of the late, great, Billy Mays: "But wait! There's more!"

Remember, this is life insurance. If you are saving for retirement and pass away unexpectedly, what happens to your family? Is there enough money in your retirement accounts to sustain them for the next 20, 30, or even 50 years? With life insurance, the ones you love most, will receive a benefit that is completely tax free. This benefit is often what was meant to save over a lifetime, or more.

If Dan and Sally were to redirect the $12,000 a year, they were contributing to their 401(k), to a properly designed cash value life insurance plan, it may look something like this:

Annual Contributions	Year	Cumulative Contributions	Cash Value	Death Benefit
$12,000	10	$120,000	$130,810	$709,244
$12,000	20	$240,000	$368,676	$1,054,691
0	30	$300,000	$718,630	$1,246,149

In this scenario, contributions are being made for 25 years, ending at age 65. If we were to look 40 years into the policy, when they are 80 years old, the cash value is projected to be north of $1.1 million. Oh, and remember, they have access to these funds without a single penny of taxes coming out! Talk about a powerful plan.

Chapter Eight: Big Banks & Wall St.

When it comes to Wall St. and the banking system, most of us understand very little of how they operate. While we know about mutual funds, the New York Stock Exchange, checking and savings accounts, and CDs, there are so many more complex operations at work. Oh, did I mention they use our money to do them?

Let's begin with a CD. What is a CD exactly? CD stands for Certificate of Deposit and how they work is simple. You could simply walk into a bank, give them a lump sum of money, and in exchange for you agreeing to not touch it for a period of time, the bank will pay you an interest rate that is higher than a savings account.

CDs can mature anywhere from 6 months to five years. Typically, the longer one is willing to lock their money in, the higher the interest rate. For example, a 6 month CD may pay .30% while a 2 year CD could pay .55% in interest. Note that this interest is taxable every year.

Helen, who has been retired for several years and is 75 years old, holds a portion of her savings in CDs. **Her biggest concern is running out of money,** and she figures by locking it up for a period of time, she won't be able to touch the money.

She currently has $200,000 in an 18 month CD. Her local bank pays 0.45% interest. What anyone in the bank doesn't explain to her is that because inflation is close to 3%, she is actually losing purchasing power every year! A representative at a bank will almost never mention this for a couple of reasons.

First and foremost, the people working in the bank have no idea how economics really work. The people working in the bank might not be interested in learning, as it is not in their scope of work, or the banks themselves intentionally keep the employees in the dark.

You may be wondering, why would they do that? The reason is simple. The banking system consists of something called fractional reserve banking. What this means is that only a fraction of deposits is backed by actual cash that are available for withdrawal.

In other words, the bank can now take Helen's locked up $200,000 and lend it out eight more times for example. So, where do banks loan this money? Remember, banks are also in the mortgage business. As this is being written, a 30 year mortgage usually has an interest rate from 3% to 4.5%, assuming decent credit.

Banks also rake in billions of dollars on credit cards and other fees. Credit cards generally charge double digit interest rates. As far as fees, well one of the biggest money makers banks have are overdraft fees. In fact, banks charged $12.4 billion in overdraft fees in 2020, according to a Forbes article written by Kelly Anne Smith in April of 2021. Pretty disgusting right?

In addition, banks are regularly fined due to their unlawful activities and violations. These activities include mis-selling of products, market manipulation, opening accounts without customer approval, and even being negligent with money laundering.

In 2020, banks worldwide amassed fines of over $15 billion, with the United States being 73% of those fines, which amounts to $11.11 billion. These fines are not only expected to continue over the years, but also rise.

So, why do I tell you all of this? It's simple, if they can take Helen's $200,000, and loan it out eight more times, that is $1,600,000. The banks are actually earning 3%-4.5% on mortgages and double digits on credit cards, and all they pay

Helen is 0.45% on her $200,000. This is how they rake in billions off our backs.

Let's move on to Wall St., which by the way is not only in bed with big banks but often the same companies. Think about who the biggest banks are. You have Wells Fargo, which has Wells Fargo Advisors. Then there is Merrill Lynch, which is owned by Bank of America. J.P Morgan Chase has a huge Wall St. presence and Bank of New York Mellon has more than $35.3 trillion in assets in custody.

These firms sell people CDs, pay as low of an interest rate as they possibly can, so they can turn around and loan the money multiple times and earn billions of dollars. These companies, along with others, control the mutual fund market as well. That's right! If you own mutual funds, there's a strong possibility one of the above named companies has your money. Then through these mutual funds, you are being charged management fees, 12b-1 fees, sales loads, redemption fees, among other expenses. **If these funds are in a retirement account, they could be north of 2% every year!**

Put another way, if the stock market is up 10%, you earn 8%. If the stock market is down 10%, your account value goes down by 12%. In other words, win, lose, or draw, Wall St. gets paid.

Wall St. and big banks make billions upon billions of dollars, and they do it all with our money. Isn't that amazing? Then, they use a large portion of their assets and place it into risky investments, like CMOs (Collateralized Mortgage Obligations), which was pivotal in the recession of 2007-2008.

After they lost trillions and brought the economy to its knees, they were deemed, "too big to fail." What does this mean? It means the government bailed them out, with our tax dollars! **The big banks received over $700 billion of taxpayer dollars.**

During this time, people lost jobs, their homes, life savings, and families were even ripped apart, and yet, Wall St. and the big banks were bailed out with our money. What did they do with our money? Well, they bought back their own stock, paid themselves hefty bonuses, and took lavish trips on private jets.

Are these the type of companies you want to place your hard earned money with? Is this who you want to borrow from? Are you concerned it could happen again? I know I am very concerned about our fragile economy, especially since I am writing this during the COVID-19 pandemic.

Want to hear the real kicker? Are you aware that **banks own more than $190 billion in cash value life insurance?** Go figure! Did you realize they own nothing, as far as I know, of what they sell us?

What is on their books? How many millions in CDs do they own? Wonder what their mutual fund portfolio looks like? A CD is just another way for the institution to capture our money so they can loan it out 8-10 times and earn multiples of interest on the money, all while having zero skin in the game.

I recently read a report on some of the largest banks, and their life insurance holdings, so allow me to break them down for you here:

Bank of America has more money in cash value life insurance than all the value of its 5600 branches and their skyscraper, which is only 50 feet shorter than the Empire State Building, making it the eighth tallest building in New York City.

Citi Bank has about $6 billion in cash value life insurance and less than $5 billion in other assets.

J.P. Morgan Chase has approximately $11 billion in cash value life insurance.

Wells Fargo holds over $19 billion of cash value life insurance.

The list goes on and on. I am quite sure by now you get the point. You know what's ironic? While they use entertainers, like Dave Ramsey, to push 401(k) plans, mutual funds, while telling us how bad cash value life insurance is, they own almost $200 billion worth.

Why don't they want us to know about this? I will tell you exactly why:

Fractional Reserve Banking

Chapter Nine: How Much Do I Need for Retirement?

Have you given thought as to how much you will need in retirement? This question is very vague, so if you don't know the answer right away, it's totally understandable.

When it comes to retirement savings, is it more important to think in terms of total nest egg or how much income we can generate? Now, while the two do work together, I would like to outline why allocation matters.

Mary is 68 years old, a widow, and has one daughter. She lives off a small pension and Social Security. Mary has managed to save money for many years and now has about a $400,000 nest egg.

Mary does not need this money and would ultimately like to leave it to her daughter. Mary is also very fearful of the stock market and wants to guarantee her principal is secure.

She holds her $400,000 in a CD that she purchased at the bank. The interest rate she gets is 0.55%. At this rate, her $400,000 is generating an annual income of $2,200. **Imagine having $400,000 and only being able to generate $2,200 annual income!** Oh, this money is taxable as well.

Gina, who is 67 years old, has saved $200,000 over the years. Gina has allocated her savings to an annuity plan. What she did was split the savings in half, taking $100,000 and creating immediate income, and taking the other $100,000 and letting it grow for the next few years.

On the $100,000 she put toward income; she will earn just over $5,700 a year for the rest of her life! No matter what happens down the road, this income will not cease, as long as Gina is alive.

What's even better is that let's say Gina waited until she was 72 to start taking an income of $100,000 from an annuity. Since income is based on life expectancy, she could expect an annual income of $6,672. That will be a total income of $12,372 on $200,000. This is over a 6% withdrawal rate on her money!

Why aren't more people doing this with their savings? Maybe it is a lack of knowledge or understanding? Perhaps financial advisors don't want them to have this information as they will lose assets under management. If you, or someone you love, had the option to create an income that was impossible to outlive, wouldn't this be important information to have?

Now that you have the information, would you rather have $400,000 in a CD paying you $2,200 a year or $100,000 in an annuity paying $5,700 or higher every year. When you would like to learn more, please reach out to me. I am here to help you gain financial peace of mind.

I believe a properly structured cash value life insurance plan can, and should, play a very important role for a more secure retirement. We have already discussed how powerful this tool can be for other purposes, but what if I told you that you can create more cash flow during retirement?

Here is a question for you. **If you lost your job and were unemployed for the next 30 years, would this have an effect on you and your family?** You are probably thinking, DUH! of course it would. Well, let me follow up with another question then. Isn't that what retirement is?

Now, if you were to retire at age 65 and pass away at age 73, we would probably have no issues planning your retirement, will we? However, what if you live to age 94 but run out of money at age 78? What will your retirement look like then?

Do you enjoy golf? What about fishing? I know many people who aspire to travel more once retired. **How will we do the things we enjoy if we are broke?** Where will you live if you run out of money? I am a pain to live with now. I cannot imagine my children would want me living with them full time when I am older and have no money. I say this jokingly, but it is something serious to consider. We simply cannot borrow our way through retirement.

One of the main benefits of building a nest egg within a life insurance plan is that you can essentially turn that asset into never taxed money. If you recall, a 401(k), IRA, 403(b), and other plans similar, grow tax deferred. By redirecting savings from a government regulated retirement plan into a cash value life insurance plan, you now change the game from tax deferral to never taxed!

Think about it. How much longer will your money last you if you never had to pay taxes on it? This is so powerful. Think of it another way. How much easier will it be to reach your savings goals if you knew that money wouldn't be taxed?

I recently asked a new client how much income he would like to earn annually from retirement. He expressed that he would like to earn the same $60,000 he earns today. Then I asked him what kind of interest rate he thinks he could get in retirement, without putting his principal at risk. He answered that if he could get 4% interest, that would be wonderful.

From there, I mapped out what it would take to meet his goals. To continue earning $60,000 a year in retirement, at a 4% interest rate, he will have to have saved $1,500,000.

But what if taxes are higher? Isn't inflation a concern? Let's look at this for a moment. If you were earning $60,000 a year and having a total of 20% taken out for taxes, then your net income would be $48,000. If taxes were slightly higher at 25%, then your take home pay would be $45,000.

Taking the $60,000, let us now consider inflation, which is all but inevitable. The only thing we don't know is by how much. At just 3% inflation, in 20 years, it would take $96,000 to have the same purchasing power as $60,000 today. This is also assuming taxes are not higher! Taxes also erode buying power.

So, would this client really need $1,500,000 saved to earn $60,000 a year, or would he need $2,400,000 to earn $96,000? Looking at it from this perspective, are we truly saving enough? The answer for most of us is an astounding no!

But what if we didn't have to pay income taxes in retirement? This is where cash value life insurance comes into play. If $96,000 a year was required in 20 years, and the taxes taken from that income were 25%, then the net income would be $72,000.

Now, if you were to earn 4% in retirement, in order to create a tax free retirement source of $72,000 a year, you would have to have saved $1,800,000. Although this may still seem like a large number, and it is, it is also $600,000, or 25%, less you would have to save when you grow your money in a vehicle that will not be taxed!

I hope you understand how powerful cash value life insurance can be, especially when saving for retirement. Please note that these plans must be designed correctly! Make sure you have an agent who understands these concepts. If you are unsure, I am more than happy to assist you. In fact, here is my cell phone: 727-902-1083.

Just keep in mind that we are super busy with people who have read this and my other book, as well as other clients. I do promise you though that we will get back to you and get you on the schedule to chat. Just please be patient. You are welcome to call and leave a message or text me directly. Myself and those around me are on a mission to help as many people as humanly possible and that includes you!

Chapter Ten: Saving for College

Most of our children will attend some sort of higher education. While some will enroll in trade schools, many will enroll into four year schools. You know what college is? It is really expensive!

As a matter of fact, college costs have been rising much faster than what they tell us inflation is. It is no wonder why we have so many students graduating, with not only a degree, but a massive bill as well.

As of this writing, student loan debt is approaching $1.8 trillion! **This puts the average student loan debt at around $40,000 per student.** This is a huge burden on newly graduating students and for many, it will take years to pay down.

This is why so many of us begin a savings plan for our children, long before they head off to college. As parents, guardians, or grandparents, we would love to see our children graduate with little or no student loan debt. Wouldn't this give them a head start in life?

The most common way to save for a child's higher education is through the use of 529 college savings plans. These plans have become the traditional way to save money for college.

What is nice about 529 plans is one can set up an automatic monthly payment into them. They are typically invested into mutual funds, like in our retirement accounts in many ways.

These plans are funded with after tax dollars and do grow tax deferred. One of the biggest benefits to a 529 plan is that when used for qualified higher education expenses, the money, including any gains, can be taken out on a tax free basis.

When it comes to beneficiaries, 529 plans are flexible. For example, if one child decides to join the military rather than go to college, the beneficiary can easily be changed to another child or family member.

While 529 plans seem like a wonderful way to save for college, and they can be, please be aware of some real potential pitfalls that do come along with these plans.

For starters, if funds are withdrawn for anything but qualified higher education expenses, then the account owner will be subjected to a 10% IRS penalty, again, like in most government regulated retirement accounts. On top of the penalty, if there are any gains, the owner would have to pay taxes as well.

But why would someone do that? Well, there are a few reasons, and I will name two right now. What if a family has only one child and that child does not attend college? Although the beneficiary can be changed to a niece or nephew, we have found that when offered that option, the account owners are generally reluctant to do so.

What if the person funding the 529 plan becomes disabled and can't work for an extended period of time? This can create a compounded problem for the plan in place. If someone is not working, how will they be able to afford such payments? Sure, one can simply stop contributing, but isn't this whole savings plan down the tubes?

In addition, if the account owner becomes disabled and loses income, they may have to take withdrawals to pay bills and live. These are not some farfetched scenarios we are talking about here. This is a harsh reality.

Oh, one more thing I almost forgot. What if, God forbid, the account owner passes away unexpectedly? Who is going to help the child save for college then? Like with retirement accounts, when an income is lost, all savings cease.

Chapter Eleven: Home Ownership

When I talk with people, whether clients, friends, or family members, there is a common theme when it comes to our primary residence. That theme is almost everyone either strives to own a home or they already do.

Another common theme is that nobody enjoys having a mortgage. When you purchase a home, it is generally accepted that a mortgage will come along with it. I mean, unless you are independently wealthy, have an inheritance, or are gifted a mortgage free home, chances are you will have a mortgage payment for the next few decades.

It is no surprise that housing is not only our largest investment but also our largest expense. With that being said, does this mean our primary residence is an asset or a liability? The answer depends on who you ask but let me share my thoughts.

I believe our home is a liability rather than an asset. The reason I say this is simple. When I look at assets, I think of things that are cash, cash equivalents, or are easily converted into cash. An asset is also something that earns more than it costs, like a rental property for example.

When I think of liabilities, I think of expenses. Our primary residence is a prime example of a liability, financially speaking. Think about it. You have a monthly mortgage payment, property taxes, insurance, utilities, and many other costs. Over time, you will need a new roof, windows, update the kitchen and bathroom(s), and maybe even throw in a pool.

These expenses can really add up over time and will certainly eat into any appreciation the home has. The thing is, we do need a place to live, right? We want it to be enjoyable and we certainly want to feel safe in our own homes.

With that said, I am not attempting to discourage you from owning a home, but rather understand that it is more about a place to live than it is something to profit from. Don't get me wrong, there can be better times to purchase than others, while there can also be more ideal times to sell.

Okay, back to mortgages. Since 95% plus of us have a mortgage, or will at some point, let me ask you this simple question: **what is the best kind of mortgage to have?** You see, you may have a different response from the next person who reads this. In fact, if you want to have a little fun, ask your friends and family this question. I will forecast that if you ask 10 people this question, you will get about 5 different answers.

What I have learned from speaking with so many people over the past few years is that most would like to be free of their mortgage. Again, housing is typically our largest expense. So, how can we accomplish this? There are a few ways to pay your mortgage early, so let us dive on in.

Extra Payments

One of the simpler ways to pay down the mortgage early, is to simply send extra payments. While some people may send one payment a year to knock 4-5 years off, others will send more regularly in an effort to knock off 10 years of payments.

I am going to assume a $200,000, 30 year loan, at 4% interest. We will not factor in HOA fees, taxes, closing costs, etc., in an effort to keep these examples super simple.

On a 30 year, $200,000 loan, at 4% interest, the monthly payment will be $954.83. Over 30 years, the total paid into will be $343,739.01. **The interest paid to the lender will amount to $143,739.01.** Keep in mind, this is even with our low interest rate environment! In other words, this mortgage will cost over $143,000!

Whenever I sit down with someone and crunch these numbers like this, they cringe when they see the amount of interest that will be paid and immediately want to pay the loan down faster so they may save money on the interest.

John would like to knock some years off his mortgage. He figures, if he can send some extra payments, when he can afford to do so, that he will save on interest and be able to save more for retirement.

He ultimately decides to send an extra money once a year, when he receives his bonus, adding up to $1909.66. By doing this, John will knock off over 7 years of payments and save $39,610.08 in interest!

Refinance:

Mary has taken a more aggressive approach and has decided to refinance to a 15 year loan. This will lower the interest rate from 4% to 3%. Her monthly payments will go from $954.83 a month to $1,381.16. This comes out to an extra $426.33 every month and will ensure she is mortgage free in 15 years instead of 30. She will also only pay the lender $48,609.39 in interest rather than $143,739.01, a savings of $95,129.62!

As you can see, when it comes to paying the mortgage off earlier, there are options available. However, what happens when the what ifs pop up in life, as they so often do? Did you know the number one cause of bankruptcy is due to medical bills? In fact, over 65% of bankruptcies in the United States can be linked to medical bills just about every year.

So, if you ever became seriously ill, or seriously injured, like in an automobile accident, what would happen? Could you produce a paycheck? On top of a loss of income, will you be faced with a mountain of medical bills?

How many people were forced to stay home during COVID-19? Many who stayed home, were not sick, but rather deemed non-essential. Didn't many of those working people face a loss of income? Could we have another pandemic down the road? What if it is an economic crisis of another kind? **What would happen if you couldn't make those mortgage payments?**

You see, if you have a whole bunch of extra equity in your home, the lender will be quicker to foreclose on you. They do this because they are much more likely to recoup the funds lent out. So, by making extra payments, or refinancing to a shorter term loan, are you potentially placing yourself, family, and home at risk?

Another thing to consider is the equity in your home earns zero. When you factor in inflation, doesn't this mean you can actually lose buying power? The equity is just sitting there, completely idle. Whether you have 10% equity or 60% equity in your home, it will have no bearing on the value of your home. So, is having a whole bunch of equity in your home a sound financial decision?

Another Option:

A very viable third option for paying your home off early would be through, you guessed it, a properly structured cash value life insurance policy. So many people just don't understand how many ways life insurance can benefit them, but now you do.

Okay, let's go back to Mary for a moment. She was considering a 15 year loan so that she can be mortgage free in half the time and pay less interest. This was going to mean that she would have an additional $426.33 out of pocket every month.

Rather than refinancing to a shorter term, what if Mary opened a cash value life insurance plan and paid the $426.33 every month into that? By doing this, Mary will be growing her savings, rather than pumping it into her home, which earns zero interest.

Currently, if Mary maintains a 30 year mortgage, in year 20, she will have a balance of $93,668. If she contributes the

$426.33 to the life insurance plan, she is projected to have over $150,000. If Mary chooses to do so, she can take the funds out of the policy and pay off the mortgage.

Mary could also decide to not pay off her mortgage early and instead, have an extra $150,000 saved toward retirement! This would totally be her choice, and yours as well, on whether you want to be mortgage free or just continue to grow your retirement nest egg.

If this was all the life insurance offered, it would be well worth it, but now, let me tell you the rest of the story.

By contributing to a cash value life insurance policy, rather than accelerating mortgage payments, there will be sufficient death benefit to pay this mortgage off, should you pass away unexpectedly. Wouldn't it be nice to know that your family can remain in the home, if they choose, even if your income was lost forever?

What happens if you become fully disabled, whether by illness or incident, and cannot produce a paycheck? Or, what if we end up in another situation where we are forced to stay home again? Hopefully it never happens again, but now we know it is a potential reality. How could you afford to stay in your home?

With the life insurance, you have access to the cash value within the plan, with no IRS restrictions or penalties. In fact, you don't have to qualify for the funds, like with a home equity loan. You simply request, and then receive. Wouldn't it be nice to know you have several months, or even years of living expenses in an account so you can focus on healing rather than worrying how the bills will be paid?

In addition, if you were to become fully disabled, there is a rider that we almost always add, called Waiver of Premium. What Waiver of Premium will do is continue to fund the plan, when you are not able, to ensure your plan stays in place. I must ask again, **what mutual fund or other investment does this?**

Chapter Twelve: But I've Already Built My Nest Egg

Perhaps you are reading this and have already built a substantial nest egg in your retirement account. Maybe by the time this book gets into your hands, you have 25 years of 401(k) contributions. You may be wondering if it is too late to shift those assets you worked so hard to accumulate, but I am here to tell you, it isn't.

As a matter of fact, now would be ideal to pay taxes on retirement plans so they can be minimized in the future, both for you and your family. Now that you understand that governments may be the main beneficiary of these accounts, it makes perfect sense to scale out of them.

Understand, I am not telling you to take a massive distribution all at once. This would create a huge tax burden for you and send you into the highest tax bracket, potentially. What I am saying is that there are options. Options to ease out of your retirement account, so that the bulk of the money you worked so hard to save, remains in your family, and out of the hands of the Internal Revenue Service.

A married couple, over age 65, has a higher standard deduction, then a younger couple would have. This means less of your income is taxed.

If you had saved $500,000 in your retirement account, for example, you could reasonably expect 30%-40% to go to taxes. In dollars, this comes out to $150,000 - $200,000!

Alternatively, you can withdraw $50,000 annually and fund a life insurance plan. If you did this for 10 years, you would contribute $500,000 into your life insurance plan. Remember, you will have to drain your retirement account, whether you need to or not. The government wants their tax revenue. This is another reason why retirement accounts are poor estate planning vehicles.

Now, let's say as you are funding this plan over the next 10 years, you die unexpectedly. Rather than pass on $500,000 of fully taxable money to your family, you pass on $500,000 - $1,000,000 of completely tax free money. How much better off would your spouse, children, or grandchildren be if they didn't have to pay any taxes on their inheritance? Also, how would it make you feel knowing that your hard earned savings stays in the family, rather than go to the Internal Revenue Service, and other entities?

Are you aware that someone turning 65 today has about a 70% chance of needing some kind of long term care? This care is quite expensive. In fact, in today's dollars, it is about $80,000 annually, and the average time is 2 ½ years. In this scenario, it would cost $200,000.

These healthcare costs have been known to wipe out lifelong savings in just a few short years. As a matter of fact, a woman I know, who is 93 years old and in need of care, has literally run out of money. Sure, she receives Social Security and some other income, but at age 93, can no longer afford to stay in the facility that has treated her so well, and this is a woman who did well for herself in life, both financially and her health. She is now officially dependent on family to help her maintain her current lifestyle.

If you had a life insurance plan, valued at $750,000, for example, you could have access to those funds to pay for skilled nursing care. If you had to be there for 3 years, it may cost you $240,000. The death benefit of your policy would be reduced by the amount you took out for the nursing care, and when you pass away, you would still be leaving your family **$510,000 completely tax free!**

Life insurance helps you stay in control, both while alive, and from the grave. Isn't it nice to know that you can maintain full control of your assets, rather than handing over your entire life savings to governments, hospitals, and nursing homes? Does this not bring you a sense of financial peace?

On the flip side, let's say you implement this kind of strategy and never require any sort of skilled nursing care. Well, you will always have access to the cash value within your life insurance policy that could really help your money last longer, maybe even for life.

But Derek, this is my life savings and I need it to live! Worry not my friend. We have a solution for you. What if I told you there was a way, that no matter what happens, you will never run out of money? Would you want to know how to do that?

Are you aware that there are ways to guarantee yourself an income for as long as you live, no matter what happens? Imagine a scenario where, even if you ran out of money, you would never run out of income. Wall St. hates these strategies because we are, once again, taking money away from them.

So, how can we achieve guaranteed lifetime income with our savings? The answer is with annuities. Now I know we've seen conflicting commercials where annuities are bashed and others where they are praised, but don't allow them to distract you. In fact, annuities were the main way employers funded pensions for their employees for decades prior to the invention of the 401(k). This is when employers began easing their own financial burdens and employees took on more savings responsibility.

To help keep it simple for you, an annuity is **a long-term investment that is issued by an insurance company** and is designed to help protect you from the risk of outliving your income. Through annuitization, your purchase payments (what you contribute) are converted into periodic payments that can last for life.

Simple enough right? **Essentially all you are doing is purchasing yourself a pension.** The amount of money you receive annually depends on two main factors. The first, and most obvious is the amount of savings you can comfortably convert into income and second, your age.

For example, if a 65 year old male wanted to convert $100,000 into a lifetime income, he would receive roughly $5,700 a year. This is a 5.7% income base. Remember the 4% rule? What a typical advisor would tell you is to take 4% of your savings and that will give you the best chance at never running out of money. With the annuity, a 65 year old can take 5.7% and guarantee that income will never cease.

If this individual waited until they were 70, that same $100,000 would get them $6,252 annually, or 6.25%. Not a bad return in this scenario and the only risk here is that the person receiving the income passes away too soon. In this case, the payments would cease, and the funds are gone forever. For this reason, one should never place 100% of their assets into an annuity.

There are ways to hedge against this risk. For instance, if you are married and your spouse would still depend on this income should you pass, there are options to take, what is known as, a joint life payment. While the overall payments will be a little lower, they would be guaranteed if one of you is alive.

Annuities can be complicated, as there are several different kinds, companies, and strategies that are offered. Let us dive a little into a few of them.

Fixed Annuities:

A fixed annuity is the most basic of annuities. I generally liken them to CD alternatives. Basically, if you have a lump sum of money, you are just trying to preserve, a fixed annuity could be an option.

While interest rates are not attractive currently anywhere, annuities have their benefits over other vehicles. For example, if you had $100,000 you wanted to preserve and had the money in a CD, you would earn around .55% on a 2 year CD. On a 5 year CD, the interest rate might be closer to .95%. So, even though you are locking your principle up for 60 months, you are still receiving less than 1%.

With a 5 year fixed annuity, you could receive 2% or something a little more. Right here alone, with the same timeframe, you would earn double the interest. In addition, with a CD, you will receive a tax bill every year on the interest earned, while with the annuity, it grows tax deferred. **This allows you to earn more than double.**

Fixed Indexed Annuities:

Fixed indexed annuities, or FIAs, are a bit more complex than a traditional fixed annuity. The one constant between the 2 of them is that your principal is protected and will never lose money.

There are several companies that offer fixed indexed annuities, and there are a variety of choices and strategies. For the purposes of this book, I am going to keep it short and simple for you. **Fixed indexed annuities allow you to participate in the upside of the markets without the downside risk.**

While there are many ways an insurance company may offer to achieve this, the most important thing is that you have a much better chance at staying ahead of inflation if you can capture some market gains, versus if you were to just earn a fixed interest amount.

If there were a catch, I would say it is in the surrender period. With a fixed annuity, you may have a 3, 5, or 7 year surrender period, where with a fixed indexed annuity, your surrender period may be 10 years or more.

Fixed indexed annuities would be more ideal for someone with a longer time horizon and wants to grow their nest egg without worrying about losses. These can be especially beneficial for someone that changes jobs and has to roll over a retirement plan from their previous employer, or perhaps someone in their sixties that won't need access to their money for many years.

Variable Annuities:

Depending on who you speak to, variable annuities are either the answer to all your retirement needs, or an overpriced, unnecessary tool. While I do not personally offer these to my clients, I will explain them here just so you have an understanding.

With variable annuities, you are generally going to invest your money into mutual fund accounts. **This also means you assume all the risks.** While you could have unlimited upside, you can also suffer losses. This could have detrimental effects when it comes time to take an income. On the flip side, if the markets perform well, you could have a higher income that could potentially be locked in for life.

Another thing to consider with variable annuities are the expenses. These savings vehicles tend to have much higher charges than fixed indexed annuities. While an indexed annuity may cost you anywhere from 0-1%, variable annuities could cost significantly more to maintain. It is important to understand this as costs could eat away at gains.

Certain indexed and variable annuities also carry income riders. While these have a cost associated with them, they also guarantee a level of income that you can count on, regardless of how your actual money performs.

Annuities can be complicated on the surface. You may hear participation rates, cap rates, mortality costs, and a slew of other fancy terminology. It is important to find a true professional that could help you understand. Like Albert Einstein once said, "If you can't explain it to a 6 year old, you don't understand it yourself." **In other words, don't let someone try and get over on you by using a bunch of industry jargon.**

Is an annuity right for you? They could be. If you are seeking some safety and would like to know that no matter what happens, you will have a steady paycheck coming in throughout retirement, then it is definitely worth exploring. If I could be of any help, please do not hesitate to reach out.

Chapter Thirteen: Protection

One question I ask everyone I sit down with is, **"do you have a will?"** A will is one of those things we can put off until tomorrow, but you know what they say. Tomorrow never comes. Tomorrow is not promised to any of us, but a will can help keep things organized for your loved ones.

So, what exactly is a will? A will is a **legal document that coordinates the distribution of your assets after death and can appoint guardians for minor children**. A will is important to have, as it allows you to communicate your wishes clearly and precisely.

This is another piece of the puzzle that can offer you that financial peace, knowing that your wishes will be taken care of, and your children will be raised by those you know, like, and trust.

Estate planning is essential with all stages of life. Whether you are a young family or retired, there are ways to ensure you protect your financial interests. This would include your home.

The wealthiest people do a really good job when it comes to keeping assets out of their name. Why should we do it any differently? If you are a homeowner, you should at least consider putting your home into a trust.

While having a will establishes who gets your home, it doesn't prevent your home from going into probate. Probate can last from 6-9 months. During this time, rest assured, the lender will still want their mortgage payments along with having to keep current with property taxes, insurance, and HOA fees, if applicable.

This could create an unnecessary financial burden on loved ones, and even lead to potentially losing the home all together. By placing the home in a trust, it could keep the home out of your estate, allowing it to bypass probate. This will allow your loved ones to make sound financial decisions and get the home sold, if that is what is in the plans.

Another thing that could prove to be ever so important is a healthcare proxy. The advantages to having a healthcare proxy is it allows you to **appoint a person and grant to him or her the authority to make medical decisions for you in the event you are unable to express your preferences about medical treatment**.

Think about it for a moment. Imagine you ended up in a vegetative state. Without a healthcare proxy, the hospital could, in theory, keep you on life support indefinitely. This could go on for months before you pass away and end up costing your loved one's hundreds of thousands of dollars in the end.

Keep in mind also, that you have your own views and beliefs on what kind of treatments or life support you would like to receive, if it ever came down to it. If you are incapacitated and are unable to make decisions, wouldn't it be nice to know that someone would express your wishes on your behalf?

Another piece of the protection puzzle would be power of attorney. As many of us age, we may experience some sort of cognitive decline. This would be the main reason why so many scammers tend to target our senior population.

Power of attorney allows someone, on your behalf, to make decisions on finances, property, and sometimes medical care, if the person is disabled in some manner, or cannot be present to sign off on necessary legal documents for financial transactions.

Regarding wills, trusts, and powers of attorney, it is not only important to have these things in order, but to have the named person or persons be someone you absolutely trust.

Also, I am not an attorney, nor will I pretend I have extensive knowledge on these matters. What I do have is access to a network of attorneys and we help our clients by, not only helping them get their money matters in order, but by connecting them to attorneys who specialize in estate planning. Our process is super simple, and very affordable.

While there is a cost to getting a will, trust, and other documents in order, the cost of doing nothing could prove to be much greater.

Chapter Fourteen: Final Thoughts

Financial advisors, financial planners, and other professionals, do a wonderful job of complicating things. I hope that by reading this book, you now fully understand that the formula is actually quite simple.

While some advisors will attempt to wow you with charts, figures, & fancy terminology, you now know that the solutions involve saving more, creating tax efficiency, protecting your income, and maintaining full control.

Everything that is written in this book, I have learned through studying and living it. We have been broke and have had some struggles. We have had to use credit cards to pay bills. I've taken distributions from retirement accounts in the past and it cost us a lot of money in taxes and penalties.

Through our own mistakes, and then education, these simple, yet powerful financial principles were developed. Also, through my own studies, I quickly learned that many of these principles are the exact ones that high earners, and even the very wealthy follow.

This was my inspiration to become an advisor. Nobody should have to feel completely lost when faced with financial hardships. By doing things right now, weathering unknowns should be a lot easier, as you will be prepared.

If you feel swamped in credit card debt, getting rid of those debts is liberating. It was one of the best moments in our financial lives, knowing we escaped the debt trap. Once you accomplish this, you will be able to save more every month and help pave the road to a secure financial future. **This is real financial peace.**

It is my wish that this short book helped you to understand what it will take, to not only reach long term financial goals, but to help you put more money in your pocket in the short term. **Often, by just making some real simple adjustments, you can achieve total peace of mind.** Wouldn't that be amazing?

So, what's next?

Well, it's time to take action. Whether you have credit card debt or not, I can certainly find places where you can save money so that you can be more prepared for retirement and the unknowns that life will be sure to throw our way.

Although I do like selling books, I have a much higher passion for helping others. If you know of someone that has credit card debt, not saving enough, or just has general concerns about the future, give them this book. Oh, and no, I am not asking you to start asking people a bunch of abrasive questions. Just keep an ear open, and if the subject comes up, be sure to get them a copy, or at least the Amazon link to purchase it.

I have saved my clients tens of thousands of dollars in interest payments over the years. My goal is to save everyone I work with tens of thousands of dollars, or more, over their lifetime. These savings will come in the form of savings from interest, taxes, and yes, market losses.

I want to thank you for taking the time to read this book. I know you crave financial peace of mind, and by reading this book, you have taken a very important step to achieving this. The next step would be to do something about it.

I am here to help. Please do not be bashful. There is never any cost or obligation to chat.

In fact, there are a few ways you can proceed from here:

1: Email me directly: Derek@polarisfinancialnetwork.com
2: Fill out the form in this book and email or text over to me
3: My office number: 727-308-3150
   My cell phone: 727-902-1083

If I, or another member of my team do not answer, please leave a message. We will promptly get back to you.

4: If you are not ready to chat yet, visit our site at polarisfinancialnetwork.com. Here you can watch videos, subscribe to the newsletter, and get more information.

Just know that when you are ready to take control of your finances, we are ready to help you.

Confidential Form to fill out and email or text

Name_____
City & State_____
Email_____
Best Phone Number: _____
Best Time of Day to Contact You_____
Topics to Discuss:
_____Eliminating Debt
_____Saving for Retirement
_____Saving for College
_____Protecting Your Paycheck
_____Other_____

We take your privacy very seriously. Any information you provide to us, in any fashion, will not be redistributed or sold. Everything you do with us is strictly confidential.

I want to thank my wife, Erin, for her unbelievable support, both professionally and at home. You are my inspiration and I love you with all my heart. You are an amazing wife to me, and mom to our children.

Thank you to Jeremy Nason, Alex Villa, and Lew Nason from the Insurance Pro Shop, for your incredible commitment to educating, not only myself, but many other financial professionals. You bring integrity to the financial services industry.

A special thanks to Stacey Nason for helping and designing this book cover. You are a true artist.

I would also like to thank everyone I have had the pleasure of working with. Many of you are not only my clients but have become my friends.

Thank you, Van Mueller, for all you have done regarding keeping up on the economics of things so we may better prepare our clients.

And a very special thank you to you! Thank you for taking the time to read this book and I hope it was eye opening for you. As a small favor, would you mind leaving a review on Amazon? I appreciate you!

www.ingramcontent.com/pod-product-compliance
Lightning Source LLC
Chambersburg PA
CBHW070125230526
45472CB00004B/1417